THE ADVENTURES,

BIG

AND SMALL,

of:

SMALL ADVENTURES JOURNAL

A LITTLE FIELD GUIDE *for* BIG DISCOVERIES IN NATURE

BY KEIKO BRODEUR

CHRONICLE BOOKS

SAN FRANCISCO

Thank you to the great editors and designers at Chronicle without whom this journal idea would never have been conceived. I am forever indebted to Malachi who is always my number one editor and helps me with everything I make. To my wonderful mom, dad, in-laws, and sister for always lending support in every way. And many thanks to Laura for bailing me out when I was stuck.

ISBN: 978-1-4521-3650-9
Manufactured in China.

10 9 8 7 6 5 4

Chronicle Books LLC
680 Second Street
San Francisco, CA 94107

www.chroniclebooks.com

Adventure at your own risk. The publisher and author disclaim all liability from any injury that may result from the use, proper or improper, of the information contained in this journal.

CONTENTS

INTRODUCTION

Most of us spent a large part of our childhood outside. I would often run around my family's yard, pretending to be a Native American warrior princess or a ninja, wielding sticks as weapons, getting my hands and clothes dirty as I climbed in and out of bushes. My focus and imagination were linked to the natural world, even if I didn't realize it. Like most people, as I grew, play turned into work and my time became more and more relegated to the indoors. When I started my paper goods line, Small Adventure, I titled it without really knowing that the theme of the work would concern itself predominantly with the natural world. I soon realized that I missed that connection to the infinite beauty of the environment and our place inside it. Now I find that the more I learn about the intricate science of the world, the more my fulfillment and happiness grow.

It's no secret that balancing our time between the rigors of daily life and moments of contemplation in the outdoors is extremely important for our health and sanity. A shift in surroundings invites engagement; it activates and opens us up a little. Then the solitude of nature can imbue personal reflection, while nature's grandeur reminds us of our context. The activities and reference materials in this journal are meant to encourage you to step into those moments of quiet, appreciation, happiness, and amazement. Flip to any page to start. You'll find exercises for exploring the outdoors whether you live in a city, the suburbs, or the country, whether you have a day or a minute. Take rubbings of different textures, draw the stars, or go on a picnic—each activity will expand your ability to see, hear, smell, and observe the natural details around you all the time. Treat this journal like a personalized field guide, not just to follow along with the prompts, but to record whatever thoughts spring up, to pursue trails created by your own imagination and experiences. My hope is that this journal will bring some stimulation and a bit of fun to your daily life, just like a kid playing in the backyard.

CHECKLIST:
OUTDOOR CLOTHING

[ ] Moisture-wicking T-shirts

[ ] Moisture-wicking underwear

[ ] Pants

[ ] Long-sleeve shirts (for sun, bugs)

[ ] Sun-shielding hats

[ ] Bandana

[ ] Boots or shoes suited to terrain

[ ] Socks (synthetic or wool)

[ ] Insulating jacket or vest

[ ] Gloves or mittens

[ ] Hiking stick

[ ] Sunglasses

[ ] Easy to carry pack

[ ] Whistle

MAP YOUR WORLD

There can be a lot of surprises tucked inside familiar territory. Take a walk around your neighborhood and draw your own map. What new things and places did you discover? Mark in your old favorite spots too. Do you have a nearby restaurant you regularly visit? A favorite tree to sit under and read?

STOP AND LISTEN

Throughout the course of one day, go outside a couple times during daylight and again at night. Listen to the different sounds around you. Do you only hear some sounds at certain times? Make note of which sounds you can hear the whole day and which you can hear only at night.

TAKE A BREATH

During your next few walks, take note of the natural smells around you
(for example: dewy grass, wet wood, dry leaves, varieties of flowers).
Decide on four favorites, and collect samples or draw them here. Occa-
sionally, bring some favorite scents that you've discovered into your
home. Having your favorite natural smells around you will make you
feel fresh and relaxed and will motivate you to spend more time outside
breathing in the scented air.

SEE THE SMALL

Wandering through a wooded area, draw all the teeny-tiny things you can find, like clovers, seeds, ants, and pebbles.

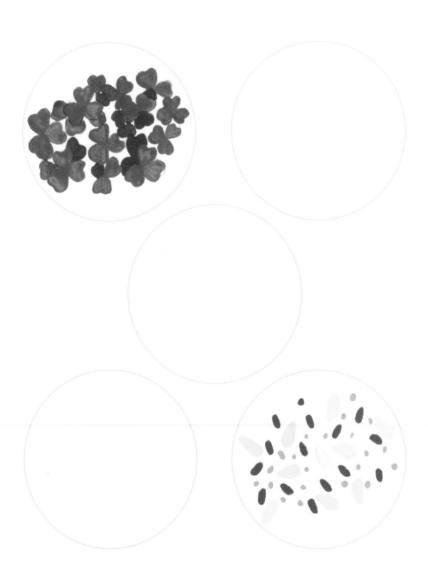

COMMON MAP SYMBOLS

SECONDARY ROADS

WOODS

DIRT ROADS / TRAILS

 SWAMP / MARSH

RAILROAD

 GRASSLAND

BRIDGE

 SAND

SCHOOL

 HILL

CHURCH

MINES

CEMETERY

 RICE PADDY

WINDMILL

CULTIVATED LAND

MEDICAL

x-x-x-x-x **FENCES**

LAKE

⊢⊢⊢⊢⊢ **TELEPHONE LINES**

SPRING

 BUILDINGS

Build a Fire

TEPEE METHOD

LOG CABIN METHOD

STAR METHOD

LEAN-TO METHOD

CROSS-DITCH METHOD

PYRAMID METHOD

CHANGE YOUR ROUTE

For one week, take a different route every day to school or work. What new things do you observe along the way?

MAKE A
SPORE PRINT

WHAT YOU'LL NEED:

- A mature mushroom* (young ones haven't dropped their spores or gills low enough to make a print)

- A piece of paper (try to use dark paper for a light-colored mushroom and light paper for a dark-colored mushroom to yield the best results)

- A cup or bowl

- A knife

On your next walk, look for a mushroom that is mature. Cut the stem off the mushroom. Notice the gills/spores underneath the mushroom cap.

Place the spores face down on the paper and cover the mushroom cap with a cup or bowl to keep air currents away. Leave this setup overnight.

In the morning, remove the cup and lift the mushroom cap. There should be a print left of the mushroom spores. Because mushrooms are best identified by their spores, this process is often used to find out the specific type of mushroom.

Try using lots of different kinds of mushrooms and placing them all around your paper to create a patterned print.

PERCEIVE THE PASSING SEASONS

When seasons change there is often something palpable in the air, whether it be a smell, a drastic temperature difference or simply a feeling you have. The next time a change of season is approaching, try to document the date when you noticed a definite change. What was it that brought your attention to the new season? A different smell in the air? The leaves taking on a new hue? Something more indefinable?

IDENTIFY THE CLOUDS

On a day with blue skies and big puffs of clouds, see if you can figure out what type they are using this reference. Take note of where and when each variety floats on by.

DATE	CLOUD TYPE

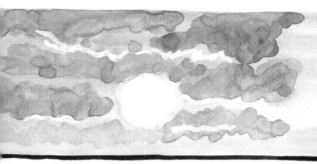

ALTOSTRATUS

or
CURTAIN
CLOUDS

CIRROSTRATUS

or
TANGLED WEB

CIRROCUMULUS

or
MACKEREL

CIRRUS
or
FEATHER

STRATUS

or
SPREAD SHEET

CUMULUS
or
WOOL PACK

STRATOCUMULUS
or
TWIST CLOUDS

CUMULONIMBUS
or
THUNDERSTORM

NIMBUS
or
UMBRELLA

ALTOCUMULUS
or
SHEEP

DATE	CLOUD TYPE

Edible Plants

ACORNS

ELDERBERRIES

CRANBERRIES

BAYBERRY

CACTUS

DANDELION

MAPLE SEEDS

HAZELNUT

MINER'S LETTUCE

CLOVER

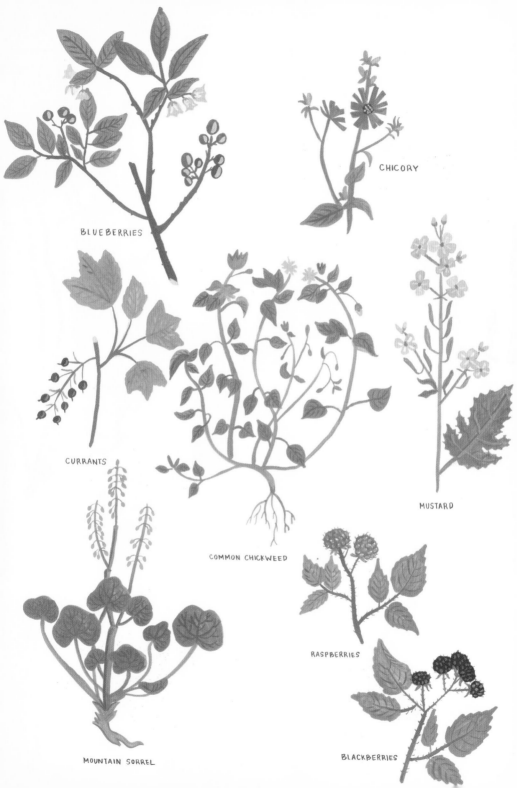

BLUEBERRIES

CHICORY

CURRANTS

COMMON CHICKWEED

MUSTARD

MOUNTAIN SORREL

RASPBERRIES

BLACKBERRIES

PHOTOGRAPH TEXTURES

Take a close-up photograph of something smooth, something rough, something soft, something prickly, and something brightly colored.

PACK A PICNIC

When was the last time you ate outdoors?
Get inspired by a sunny day and take
some of your favorite foods outside to a
nearby park or your front lawn. Do you
find that you notice the flavors in your
food more than if you ate hastily inside?
Try eating different foods outdoors
and see what your favorites
might be.

Favorite outdoor foods:

_____

_____

_____

_____

_____

_____

_____

LISTEN TO THE LIVING

What animal or insect noises do you hear in your area on a regular basis? Birds chirping, bears growling, coyotes howling? Are there animal or insect sounds you didn't realize were going on around you before?

[ ] Absorbent compress dressings

[ ] Adhesive bandages

[ ] Adhesive cloth tape

[ ] Antibiotic ointment packets

[ ] Antiseptic wipe packets

[ ] Aspirin packets

[ ] Breathing barrier

[ ] First aid instruction manual

[ ] Hydrocortisone ointment packets

[ ] Instant cold compress

[ ] Oral thermometer

[ ] Non-latex gloves

[ ] Roller bandage

[ ] Scissors

[ ] Space blanket

[ ] Sterile gauze pads

[ ] Triangular bandages

[ ] Tweezers

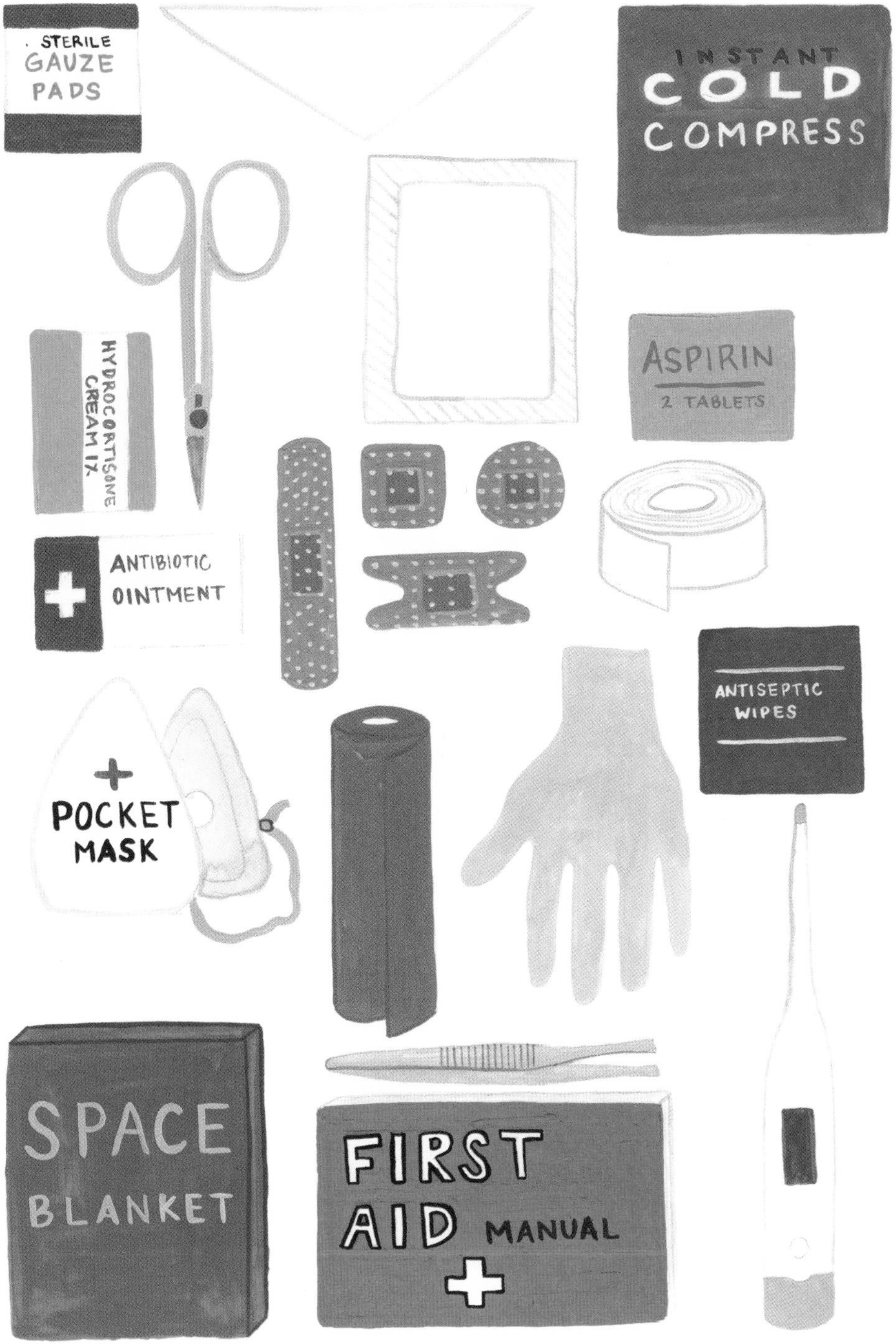

STERILE
GAUZE
PADS

INSTANT
COLD
COMPRESS

HYDROCORTISONE
CREAM 1%

ASPIRIN
2 TABLETS

ANTIBIOTIC
OINTMENT

ANTISEPTIC
WIPES

+
POCKET
MASK

SPACE
BLANKET

FIRST
AID MANUAL
+

MAKE A
SMUDGE STICK

WHAT YOU'LL NEED:

• A variety of herbs, such as sage, rosemary, and lavender, or just one kind of herb is okay too

• Scissors

• String

• Matches

Smudge sticks are traditionally used to cleanse a sacred space but they are also an effective way to bring natural scents into your home. Plus it's rewarding to forage for materials or ingredients to use in a project.

Favorite herb combinations:

Trim herbs, keeping their leafiest parts, to make them about 6–10 in./10.16–25.4 cm.

Bundle herbs together as shown and use cotton twine to firmly tie the bundle in a crisscross pattern.

Hang sticks up to dry fully.

When dry, use your smudge stick by lighting one end and fanning it around the room to disperse its scent.

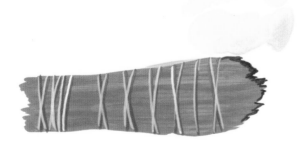

TEST YOUR SENSE OF TOUCH

Our sense of touch is sometimes deceiving. Next time you're hanging out with friends, collect some natural objects you find outside and blindfold one person. See if they can figure out what each object is by touching them. For a challenge, try using objects that have similar textures so the blindfolded person has to rely on other knowledge besides just texture.

Objects that tickled me:

NOTICE THE UNUSUAL

Uncommon occurrences happen all the time around us and often go unnoticed. Use this space to document a few rare moments you notice: Did you see two butterflies at once chasing each other and flitting around in the cold of winter? A shooting star? A dog cuddling with a cat?

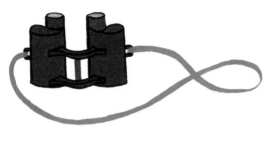

KNOT TYING

overhand knot

bowline knot

figure eight knot

1.

2.

3.

clove hitch knot

square knot

carrick bend knot

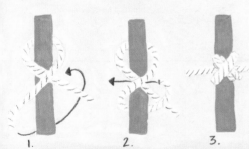

1.

2.

3.

constrictor hitch knot

sheet bend knot

granny knot

1.

2.

3.

4.

anchor bend knot

TAKE TEXTURE RUBBINGS

Use this page to take rubbings of different textures in your area: rocks, bark, leaves, cement, brick, or shells. Hold a pencil so the flat side of the lead is against the paper. Press the paper up against the object you're going to rub against and evenly rub the pencil across the page to get an image of the texture.

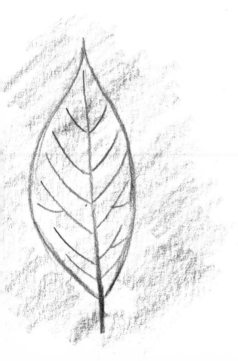

BIRD-WATCH

While on a walk, identify some of the common birds you see using this reference. Is it a robin? A parrot? A sparrow? Sketch or make a list of which birds you see here.

DUCK

SPARROW

QUAIL

WREN

GOOSE

BLUEBIRD

ROBIN

HUMMINGBIRD

TURKEY

MAGPIE

PUFFIN

WARBLER

PARAKEET

PIGEON

OWL

CHICKADEE

FINCH

SWAN

CRANE

STARLING

KOOKABURRA

LOOK DOWN

What kinds of ground do you cross as part of your daily routine? Asphalt, cement, dirt, grass, brick, cobblestone, sand? Take off your shoes and feel the different kinds of ground with your bare feet.

LOOK UP

What lies above and beyond your normal field of vision?
What shapes of light do the leaves in trees create?
How do the lines of the cityscape bisect the sky?

ANIMAL TRACKS

RACCOON

OTTER

RABBIT

MOOSE

MOUSE

BEAR

BEAVER

COYOTE

BOB CAT

DOG

DEER

TURKEY

SQUIRREL

MUSKRAT

TRAIL SIGNS

STONES	STICKS	LONG GRASS	PEBBLES
THIS IS THE TRAIL	THIS IS THE TRAIL	THIS IS THE TRAIL	THIS IS THE TRAIL
 TURN RIGHT	TURN RIGHT	TURN RIGHT	TURN RIGHT
TURN LEFT	TURN LEFT	TURN LEFT	TURN LEFT
DANGER / WARNING	DANGER / WARNING	 DANGER / WARNING	DANGER / WARNING

BE PREPARED

List or draw your ideal group of daily items that you carry with you or would like to carry with you. There are, of course, the usual things that most people can't be without—keys, wallet, phone—but what else would make you feel more prepared or aid you in a spontaneous moment of inspiration? For example, a deck of playing cards for instant fun with friends or new acquaintances, a small camera for when the light hits the Earth in just the perfect way, or a travel pack of colored pencils to doodle in this book when you have a spare moment.

MATCH COLORS

Create a swatch page of the natural colors around you using whatever medium you'd like (colored pencils, paint, or pastels are good options). Try to get your colors as close to the original as possible.

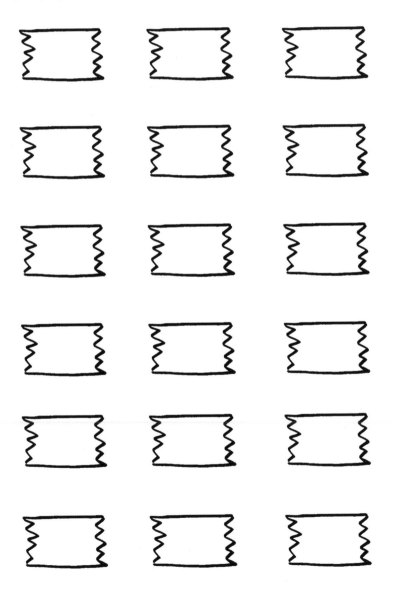

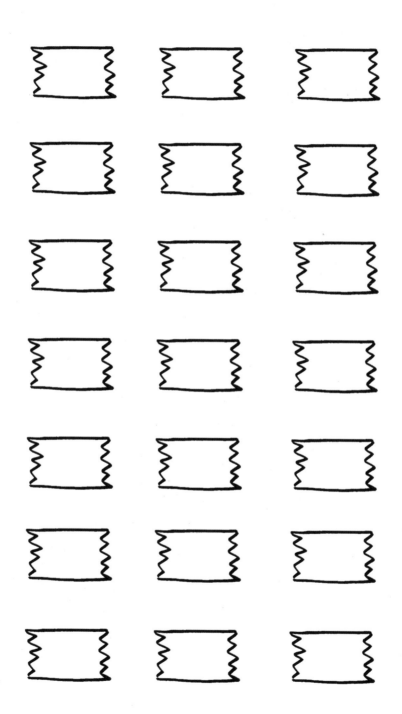

ursa major

cassiopeia

lyra

draco

orion

scorpio

STUDY THE STARS

Draw a map of the main constellations you see tonight and document the date. A month from now draw another constellation map and compare it to your first map. What moved or changed? Use this reference as a guide to pinpoint some commonly seen constellations.

MONTH

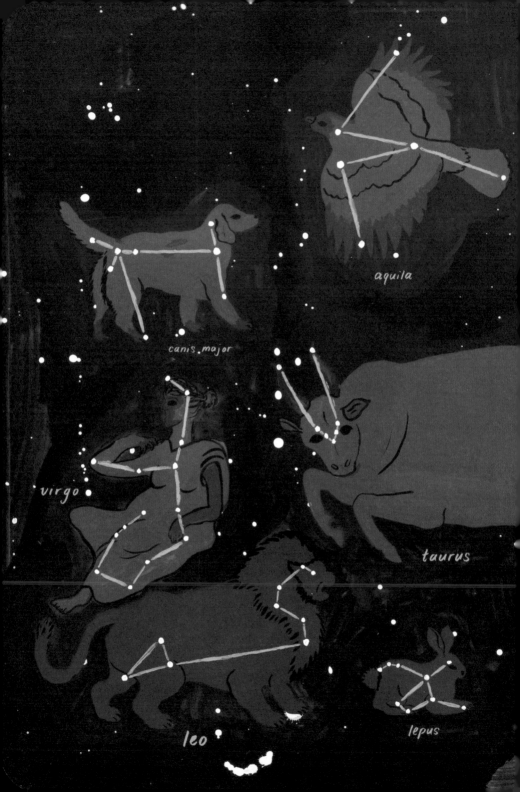

aquila

canis major

virgo

taurus

leo

lepus

MONTH

OBSERVATIONS:
What moved or changed?

CHECKLIST:
BEST FOODS AND TOOLS FOR HIKING

[ ] Trail mix

[ ] Dried fruits

[ ] Tuna

[ ] Crackers

[ ] Energy bars or granola bars

[ ] Jerky

[ ] Water

[ ] Cheese sticks

[ ] First aid kit

[ ] Flashlight

[ ] Compass

[ ] Pocket knife

GO TREE SPOTTING

While it may seem infantile to identify trees just like you used to do in your early school years, revisiting this basic information can be just as interesting as it once was. What kinds of trees grow in your local area?

TREE TYPE	LOCATION

ALDER

BEECH

DOUGLAS FIR

EUCALYPTUS

MAPLE

HAZEL

ELM

CYPRESS

ASH

SPRUCE

CEDAR

POPLAR

OAK

SYCAMORE

PALM

PINE

TREE TYPE	LOCATION

MAKE A
SLING SHOT

WHAT YOU'LL NEED:

- 1 Y-shaped branch

- 1 or 2 wide rubber bands (about ¼ in./0.63 cm wide)

- 1 oval-shaped piece of scrap leather (about 3 ½ x 2 in./ 8.89 x 5.08 cm) or whatever you think fits the best with the size of your branch)

- Scissors

- A knife

- Skinny string or dental floss

Look for a Y-shaped branch on your next adventure. To make a sling shot, first cut down your Y-shaped branch to be about 8 in./20.3 cm in length. The forks of your branch should be about 4 in./10 cm long for best results. Use the knife to trim any bumps or knots in the wood, which will make holding your sling shot more comfortable. Cut grooves around both forks about ¼ in./0.63 cm down from the top. This will keep your string in place.

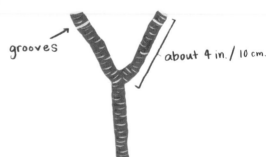

grooves

about 4 in. / 10 cm.

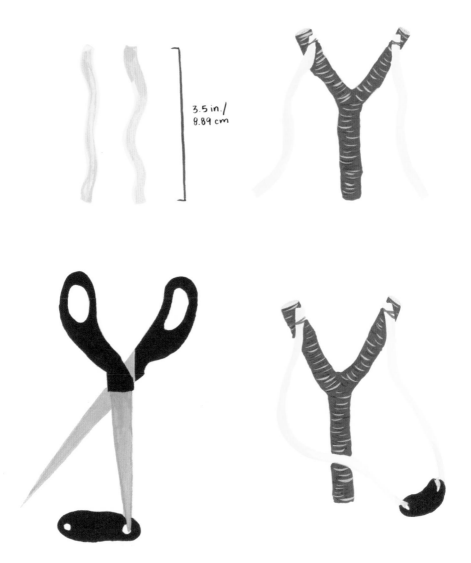

3.5 in./
8.89 cm

Cut the rubber bands into 2 pieces each about 3½ in./8.89 cm long. Attach the rubber bands over the tips of your sling shot handle using string or floss. Tie it as tight as you can while keeping the string inside the grooves. Take your scissors and punch 2 holes into the widest ends of the scrap leather. Using the string, tie the scrap of leather to the loose ends of the rubber bands that are attached to the sling shot.

COLOR THE SKY

On the next sunny day, document the various colors in the sky from morning to night by taking photographs or painting swatches. Title each color as you see fit. Is it robin's egg blue? Electric orange-pink? Melancholy gray?

DRAW THE HORIZON

Draw the horizon view from your home each morning for a week. Try to capture where the sun rises and make note of what time it rises. What do you notice?

EXAMPLE

MAY 5
6:00 AM

MAY 6
5:59 AM

MAY 7
5:58 AM

MAY 8
5:57 AM

DRAW YOUR HORIZON

MAY 9
5:57 AM

MAY 10
5:56 AM

MAY 11
5:55 AM

MORSE CODE

A ·—	N —·	1 ·————
B —···	O ———	2 ··———
C —·—·	P ·——·	3 ···——
D —··	Q ——·—	4 ····—
E ·	R ·—·	5 ·····
F ··—·	S ···	6 —····
G ——·	T —	7 ——···
H ····	U ··—	8 ———··
I ··	V ···—	9 ————·
J ·———	W ·——	0 —————
K —·—	X —··—	
L ·—··	Y —·——	
M ——	Z ——··	

FLAG SIGNALS

TAKE A
SPECIMEN PRESSING

WHAT YOU'LL NEED:

- A plant or flower specimen of your choosing

- Newspaper (2 pieces at first, and then more for switching out during the drying process)

- Corrugated cardboard (2 pieces)

- Scrap wood (2 pieces)

- Heavy books, bricks, or a belt

Cut all your materials (newspaper, cardboard, wood) to about the same size (the size doesn't really matter as long as all the materials are uniform) and make sure they're at least a bit bigger than your specimen.

Choose your plant or flower and brush off any dirt and blot any moisture.

Arrange the specimen however you'd like on one of the pieces of newspaper and place the other piece of newspaper on top.

Put the newspaper/specimen sandwich inside two pieces of cardboard, and then place the whole package between two pieces of scrap

wood. Finally, secure your specimen press pile using a belt or heavy books or bricks.

Check your specimen every couple of days to make sure no mold is growing inside and replace the damp newspapers with dry sheets. It will take about 2–4 weeks for your specimen to dry completely.

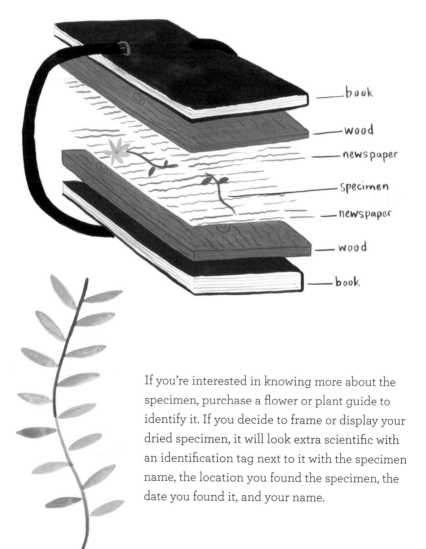

- book
- wood
- newspaper
- specimen
- newspaper
- wood
- book

If you're interested in knowing more about the specimen, purchase a flower or plant guide to identify it. If you decide to frame or display your dried specimen, it will look extra scientific with an identification tag next to it with the specimen name, the location you found the specimen, the date you found it, and your name.

CATCH MOVEMENTS (BINGO)

Try to find a whole row or column of these motion themed occurrences.
Play this with a friend on a road trip or by yourself to see how many you
can spot.

PLAYER

BINGO

SMALL RODENT SCUTTLING	LAUNDRY DRYING IN THE BREEZE	CAR	BEETLES	KIDS RUNNING
TRAIN	TRAVELING CLOUDS	DARTING LIZARD	SAUNTERING CAT	AIRPLANE
LEAVES RUSTLING	FLOCK OF BIRDS	BUTTERFLY	FISH SWIMMING	DOG WALKER
HUMMINGBIRD	BICYCLIST	ANIMAL CLIMBING IN A TREE	SHOOTING STAR	ANIMALS CHASING EACH OTHER
FLYING BALLOON	BEE	RUNNING WATER	LINE OF ANTS	BACKPACKER

BINGO

FISH SWIMMING	BACKPACKER	KIDS RUNNING	ANIMALS CHASING EACH OTHER	BUTTERFLY
TRAVELING CLOUDS	DARTING LIZARD	HUMMINGBIRD	SMALL RODENT SCUTTLING	BEE
ANIMAL CLIMBING IN A TREE	CAR	FLYING BALLOON	SHOOTING STAR	LEAVES RUSTLING
BEETLES	AIRPLANE	RUNNING WATER	LAUNDRY DRYING IN THE BREEZE	FLOCK OF BIRDS
BICYCLIST	LINE OF ANTS	TRAIN	SAUNTERING CAT	DOG WALKER

POISONOUS MUSHROOMS

FLY AGARIC

CLUSTERED WOODLOVER

DEADLY CONOCYBE

YELLOW HOUSE PLANT

IVORY FUNNEL

DEATH CAP

DEADLY GALERINA
AKA
AUTUMN SKULLCAP

DEADLY PARASOL

DAPPERLING

DESTROYING ANGEL

FALSE MORELS

MAKE A
TIME CAPSULE

WHAT YOU'LL NEED:

• A jar, thermos, or shoe box

• Collected objects

• Shovel or gardening trowel (optional)

Collect beautiful or meaningful treasures from your next walk or adventure, and store them in a jar, thermos, or shoe box. If you think it might benefit someone who finds your time capsule in the future, feel free to bury it or hide it. Otherwise keep it for yourself to open at a later date of your choosing.

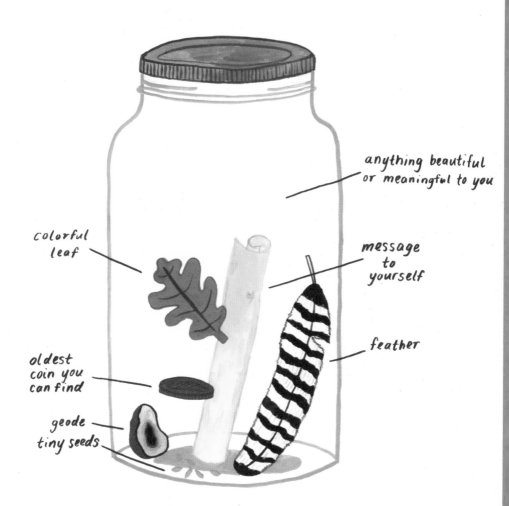

anything beautiful
or meaningful to you

colorful
leaf

message
to
yourself

feather

oldest
coin you
can find

geode
tiny seeds

FOLLOW THE MOON

Using these little calendars, draw the phase of the moon for each night of the month. Repeat on the following pages for up to five months if you'd like to observe even more.

LAST QUARTER

WANING CRESCENT

WANING GIBBOUS

NEW MOON

FULL MOON

WAXING CRESCENT

WAXING GIBBOUS

FIRST QUARTER

MONTH

1	2	3	4	5	6	7
8	9	10	11	12	13	14
15	16	17	18	19	20	21
22	23	24	25	26	27	28
29	30	31				

OBSERVATIONS:

What do you notice?

MONTH

1	2	3	4	5	6	7

8	9	10	11	12	13	14

15	16	17	18	19	20	21

22	23	24	25	26	27	28

29	30	31

OBSERVATIONS:
What do you notice?

[   ]

MONTH

1	2	3	4	5	6	7

8	9	10	11	12	13	14

15	16	17	18	19	20	21

22	23	24	25	26	27	28

29   30   31

OBSERVATIONS:
What do you notice?

MONTH

1	2	3	4	5	6	7

8	9	10	11	12	13	14

15	16	17	18	19	20	21

22	23	24	25	26	27	28

29	30	31

OBSERVATIONS:
What do you notice?

MONTH

1	2	3	4	5	6	7

8	9	10	11	12	13	14

15	16	17	18	19	20	21

22	23	24	25	26	27	28

29	30	31

OBSERVATIONS:
What do you notice?

CHECKLIST:
CAMPING GEAR

- [ ] Tent
- [ ] Sleeping bag
- [ ] Foam or air mattress
- [ ] Travel pillow
- [ ] Backpack
- [ ] Headlamp or flashlight, with spare battery
- [ ] Maps, compass (make sure you can read them before you set out)
- [ ] After-sun treatment, such as aloe vera gel
- [ ] Lightweight trekking towel
- [ ] Toothbrush, toothpaste, floss
- [ ] Survival blanket

- [ ] Snakebite kit, where appropriate
- [ ] Knife
- [ ] 3.2 yd./3 m length of rope
- [ ] Lighter (at least one), gas or petrol, plus a small pack of storm matches (can be a lifesaver in heavy rain)
- [ ] Wet wipes
- [ ] Waterproof stuff sacks
- [ ] Small shovel (optional, if your pack weight is too heavy)
- [ ] Lantern
- [ ] Whistle
- [ ] Cyalume glow-stick
- [ ] Emergency flare

- [ ] Camera, film
- [ ] Notepad and pen for journaling
- [ ] Stove
- [ ] Windscreen
- [ ] Fuel
- [ ] Fuel bottle(s) with fuel funnel
- [ ] Matches
- [ ] Charcoal
- [ ] Firewood
- [ ] Saw
- [ ] Axe
- [ ] Grill rack
- [ ] Frying pan
- [ ] Cook pots
- [ ] Pot holder
- [ ] Dutch oven

- [ ] Hot–cold vacuum bottle
- [ ] Hand-crank blender
- [ ] Bottle opener/corkscrew
- [ ] Can opener
- [ ] Recipes
- [ ] Marshmallow/wiener roasting sticks
- [ ] Food storage containers
- [ ] Resealable storage bags
- [ ] Trash bags
- [ ] Tablecloth and clips (or tape)
- [ ] Coolers
- [ ] Ice
- [ ] Water bottles
- [ ] Plates, bowls, mixing bowls
- [ ] Measuring cups
- [ ] Utensils
- [ ] Paring knife

- [ ] Spatula
- [ ] Cutting board or cutting surface
- [ ] Funnel
- [ ] Foil
- [ ] Biodegradable soap
- [ ] Collapsible water container(s)
- [ ] Portable or standing camp sink
- [ ] Quick-dry towels
- [ ] Toilet paper
- [ ] Sunscreen
- [ ] Lip balm
- [ ] Insect repellent
- [ ] Hand sanitizer
- [ ] Alcohol or antiseptic wipes
- [ ] First aid kit (see First Aid Checklist)
- [ ] Brush/comb

Other:

_____

_____

_____

_____

_____

_____

_____

_____

_____

_____

_____

_____

_____

_____

ADVENTURES TO GO ON

Keep up your motivation to go on adventures by making a list
of goals you now have for your future enterprises. Do you want to
travel to Canada to see the aurora borealis? Or scuba dive in the
Great Barrier Reef? Or maybe you'd rather learn to fish or ski?
The possibilities for adventure are endless!

NOTES